ANOTHER LANGUAGE

ANOTHER LANGUAGE

new and selected poems by

Joseph Murphy

SHANTI ARTS PUBLISHING
BRUNSWICK, MAINE

ANOTHER LANGUAGE

Copyright © 2021 Joseph Murphy

All Rights Reserved
No part of this book may be used or reproduced
in any manner whatsoever without the prior
written permission of the publisher except
for brief quotations in critical reviews.

Published by Shanti Arts Publishing
Interior and cover design by Shanti Arts Designs

Shanti Arts LLC
193 Hillside Road
Brunswick, Maine 04011

shantiarts.com

Cover and interior image by welcomia/
istockphoto.com/515010373

Printed in the United States of America

ISBN: 978-1-956056-10-5 (softcover)

Library of Congress Control Number: 2021947642

for Frances

Contents

Acknowledgments	9

PART I

In the Green Hour	14
The Beating of Unseen Wings	15
Leaving the Path	16
Out Walking	17
Failure to See the Stars	18
Our Wings Hold Steady	20
Love Embodied	21
When the Sun Rises	22
A Dream of Dreams	23
The Second Hand	24
Breathing Freely	25
Compass	26
So Many Dreams	28
A Time for Joy	29
Wanderer	30
Fantasy	31
A Discovery	32
It's There	33
After the Rains Ended	34

PART II

Winter's End	38
The Shape of New Words	39
The Descent	40
The Seeker	41
As It Is	42
Illusions	44
The Departure	45
A Light that Clings	46
Now and Then	47
The Pressure	48
My Slender Oars	49
Times Like These	50
Crafting Wings	51
Let Death Keep	52

PART III

THAT FIRST TOUCH	56
BACK HOME	57
MAGIC	58
OUR NEW VOICES	59
ONE STEP FURTHER	60
WHAT JOINS US	61
OUR PROMISES	62
WHAT NEVER FALTERS	63
OUR SECRETS	64

PART IV

SECOND CHANCE	68
THE RUDDER	69
THE CONVERSATION	70
THE COMEDIAN	71
MESSAGES	72
FRIENDS	74
VENOM	75
THE SINGING	76
MAGICIAN	78
THE LOVER	79
THE HOPE	80
DRAWING TOWARD YOU	81
BREAKING POINT	82
THE ALIEN	83
SURROUNDED	84
TAKE MY HAND	85
A NEW BEGINNING	86
INESCAPABLE	87
NEVER AGAIN	88
YOUR CHALICE	89
FULL CIRCLE	90

ENVOI

ANOTHER POEM	94
ABOUT THE AUTHOR	97

Acknowledgments

Grateful acknowledgment is made to the editors of the following publications in which many of these poems originally appeared:

Alliterati
Amethyst Arsenic
Amethyst Review
Ariel Chart
Bryant Literary Review
Burningword Literary Journal
Chantarelle's Notebook
Claudius Speaks
Clementine Colorado's Best Emerging Poets 2019
Connotation Press
Crossways Magazine
Dash
Deep Water Literary Journal
Earthspeak
Flying Catchup Press
Freshwater Literary Journal
Ginosko Literary Review
Gyroscope Review
Ink in Thirds
Living Poets
Memoryhouse
Pangolin Review
Poetry Matrix
Pure Francis
The Remington Review
SP Quill
Sprout Magazine
Strand Lit Sphere
The Stray Branch
TAB: The Journal of Poetry and Poetics

Ted Ate America
Tigershark Magazine
Third Street Writers "Lost and Found" Anthology
Twisted Vines Literary Arts Journal
Vox Poetica
Waterways
Whistling Fire
Wilderness House Review
Writer's Cafe Magazine
Writer's Circle "Ends" Anthology

The poems in Part 2 and Part 3 were later collected in a chapbook, *Crafting Wings*, Scars Publications, 2017.

The poems in Part 4 were written during the author's twenties, 1973–1979. He later found them in a folder lodged in the back of a file cabinet and began writing again after an approximately twenty-year hiatus. Having made very few changes, he began submitting the poems for publication in late 2017, and a number have subsequently been published. The author hopes that those who read these poems will have had less turbulent decades and never lose faith in their work.

PART I

"To say what you want to say, you must create another language and nourish it for years with what you have loved, with what you have lost, with what you will never find again."

—George Seferis

In the Green Hour

—after Gottfried Benn

In the green hour
silence illuminates a shrouded hope—
offers us a towering shadow,
a gleaming wing.

A song begins to emerge from our mingled voices
as we enter the deep green. The chain that held us back,
has fallen away. From our landing place—
such vastness!

The intensity of the light
at first frightens us, but we move ahead
through love and danger; regret, gain.

Our words begin to blur, fuse; become part
of the fluid, deepening green.

A wish fulfilled—
our pulses meld, resonate
within root and branch, loam
and wing; submerge and resurface
in the lines of Buddha's palm.

The Beating of Unseen Wings

> *there is in me*
> *older and harder than life and more impartial,*
> *the eye that watched before there was an ocean.*
> —Robinson Jeffers

Before there was an ocean and more brilliant
than a well-dreamed sun,
a yet-to-be-spoken word
shimmered from a stone's
rigid shadow.

And before that shadow
could raise its voice, an echo
resounded in the throat
of a well-worn,
but never walked path.

And older and harder than that echo,
within each of our cells,
others' heartbeats; eyes of creatures
being birthed; stars
yet to implode.

And within our grasp
the beating
of unseen wings, the arc
of a bird's flight—but no more
than what any mountain
has held aloft
in its out-stretched hands.

Leaving the Path

That coarse evening's light
churned from the horizon; bent down
too far, shattered.

The night's cry for help
went unanswered, regret festering
from its bitter logic.

How to restart? Regain fluidity?

Looking away, I let the map
fall from my hands. Leaving the path,
I pin my hopes to a bare wall,
wanting to slow the clock; remeasure
the width of my latest dream.

Renewed, I begin to climb; view
the horizon's gleam.

The weight has lifted. My words
begin to whirl
from the veins of leaves.

Out Walking

Swaying prairie grass. Sunlight
twirling shadows
down the breadth
of a mountain's peak.

Distant voices and a swirl of dust.

A water-cut track
bordering clay outcrops, scribbled with fissures.

The clarity of a bird's call.

Beneath my feet,
a swirl of stars
tumbling in the surf.

Failure to See the Stars

—after César Vallejo

What if our hopes were strewn before us? Flung
at our feet like torn laces? What if truths
were just tokens—
oddly shaped, useless?

Would it matter if the sky
wrenched the ears from our skulls,
punctured our lungs?

When we walked out one morning
and fell to our knees,
would the shallowness of our breath matter?

Maybe the insects would be happier without us;
trees would begin to write
their own poems; the loam's voice
would be clearer, brighter.

Down at the very bottom,
where we've lined up our grievances and hatreds
waves still break
over the pebbles we haven't crushed.

At the very top, luckily, light still emerges
through the gate
that Buddha left open.

Who can see it? Feel the warmth it radiates?

How diminished we've become. A falling leaf
bruises our foreheads. Tarnished dreams
riddle our future!

So much grief.

Grief from the hollowness
of a feigned smile, from the separation
of locked arms, from a failure to see the stars
embedded within our hands.

Our Wings Hold Steady

The clock's hands
have wriggled from a nest
we'd built to contain them.

As the ticking begins, a seed
sprouts. What had been a ribbon
has became the key we'd sought.

Songs begin struggling from the surface of our dreams.

We begin to rise. Our wings hold steady
as gravity pursues us. Wordless,
we are swept above our longings,
wonder and dread
erased from our thoughts.

Love Embodied

—for Frances

When the silence came stalking,
asking for me,
you knew we'd join hands. Turn our backs
to its hollowed-out dream.

I knew you'd help carry the light,
though it weighed so little, was so fluid,
so hard to grasp.

You knew it would flood our lives: burn the silence
from our bodies; rip it
from our shadows.

Our blood wouldn't be spilled, nor our words fester.

You were—are—love, embodied.

When the Sun Rises

When the sun rises,
perhaps the living and dead
will once again join hands
in that soft, first light.

A weight will be lifted
from the shoulders of the unborn.
Once again the sea will be calm, the forest echo
with the sound of seedlings
rising from the loam.

And when the sun rises, perhaps
the long shadow of those dead and living hands
will cease to quiver; our words begin to shine
as miraculously as the universe
that birthed us.

Perhaps, when the sun rises
the sound of our words will no longer tear
through fingertip and quill; rip through oak leaf
and spinal cord.

Perhaps our voices
will be raised in unison—
once and for all
allow the tall grass
to sway freely.

A Dream of Dreams

Leaping from a cloud's palm, my dream
rose through sleet and hail,
landing in the far corner of your sleep.

It was there my dream first heard yours singing.

So many melodies! So much hope,
radiance, despair.

Our dreams began to sway
in unison, jab
at what's kept us apart.

The Second Hand

> *Names leap ahead like hunting hounds,*
> *with the belief they clear the road*
> *of the journey's unexpected obstructions.*
> —Luljeta Lleshanaku

When a mountain was reshaped by a wing,
coins fell from an emptied pocket,
and a second hand
shaped by Buddha's breath
paused.

Names leapt past me
as a gate opened
within an emptied jar. Ahead
a radiance—obscuring
thought, action, remorse.

And when the second hand
turned again, Buddha paused
at the edge of a stream,
to watch our names sprout
from the loam at his feet.

Breathing Freely

Night crept from its latest skin,
burrowing beneath a star-shaped mountain.

When it emerged, we rose
from our hiding places.
Planets we cherished
swirled above our joined hands.

We abandoned the worn, tainted memories
we'd clung to, freeing us
to reimagine our desires.

Just before sunrise,
as we lowered the night's weight from our shoulders,
we began to chant
what the sea had promised to chant with us,
once our cages were emptied
and we again
breathed freely.

Compass

—after Murilo Mendes

To the west, everything is hushed, unclouded. Seams resewn; windows reopened.

I watch as a mountain top's shadow
mutes words
death had fashioned
from the grime of its forehead.

When I speak, my words
must pass through the furrow of my memories.
When you speak,
our memories join; disembark
from fear.

So much can be seen by those who wonder.

Right here, a door is open, a book
is laid aside, and dreams
splash down the legs of my chair.

A lightening bolt has begun to shimmer
from its tattered past,
there, at your feet
as the radio plays, the fan turns.

Anything can happen for those who imagine.

In the east, along a sunny path,
mirrors reflect fabulous histories,
tenderness and love; a lost chest
is found, overflowing with messages
of devotion and praise.

What was in shadow now emanates light. Malice
is repented, wounds rectified.

To the north and south, bells ring, riderless horses
trot across the heavens:
clouds murmuring, swelling,
as women holding scented herbs look on—
as I look on;
as men clasp one another's hands;
as the world spins
along the edge of a coin.

So much beckons to those who appreciate the invisible.

How wonderful to breathe cool air, right here,
as rain falls
and shadows of the unborn
mingle on the nib of my pen.

So Many Dreams

The mountains seem to have drawn closer, brighter,
as what we have sown
begins to rise
from the crest of our entwined dreams.

So many dreams that share the same leaves,
the same bark. Dreams
pressing from dread to light; shedding
blood and sorrow.

Dreams that form a figurine at the prow of our lives
pushing us ahead, willing hope
from a dried husk; from footsteps
yet to be taken.

Our dreams charge the loam with star-bright intensity,
reshaping Buddha's silhouette.

The charge animates memories, pierces rejection.

A rose begins to ascend from a newly-framed hope.
Nothing becomes uncertain,
beyond imagining.

No road has ever been so well marked, so emptied
of remorse, regret.

We can now join hands, regardless
of our longings, our past.

A Time for Joy

I'm sifting through what might
or could be, wondering
has the time come?

What will it take? I'm finding
the ship's wheel easy to turn, but the sky
is clouding; masts
beginning to groan.

Should I have stayed on the mountain, lazing in the grass?

On one side a tower. I'm at the top, calling out,
so sure of my words. On the other side, I'm trudging
through refuse and scree.

But I have hope.

I can still endure the sunlight; sweet-talk
the restive darkness; keep shard and blade
from multiplying.

I've mastered camouflage, too.

No one can see the cracked mortar, the brittle edges,
the wobbling stride.

Everything looks fine—as it should be.

No time for a mirror-true likeness. Time only
for joy, for whatever good comes
before death.

Wanderer

1

Which way to go? Ahead,
a grassy path, a patch of sunlight.

But the sand keeps changing form. Once
a stepladder, now a peak.

Shells leap up, scorching my fingers:
the wind blares; coins
refuse to wake.

Which way to go? I drift,
anchorless; no frame
to stitch, string to tighten.

2

Finally—motionless. Sweet silence.
A clearing.

Fresh breeze, soft light. Before me,
a wooden Buddha
seeming to ascend, unfettered
by thought.

Fantasy

When I hear the mountain's voice,
words rise from a burnt page
and a door in my heart swings open.

As it opens, I unclench my fist
and begin to preen the wings I had cast aside.

I fit them into a falcon's dream: within it and aloft,
I hear the melody the loam is humming
beneath the green leaves
of your breath.

Words that rise from that burnt page
no longer need to be shunned. You've written them
on the case you carry; on the note
to your lover; on the door that's swung open
in my heart.

Words as real as the world's brow; as the wings
I had cast aside. Imagine it!

A Discovery

A friend once said...

"Did you know
a stone can flutter
in a leaf's vein; in an oak ring's
bloom?"

That's something to believe!

"Did you know a breeze
can sift the wake
of a wave's nimble shadow?"

That's something to remember!

"And did you know

       —suddenly—

a poem can dash
across your fingertips, reshape
the soft, the brittle,

remove distinctions, restore
a yearning for silence?"

How wonderful!

It's There

> *In the air, there your root remains, there, in the air.*
> —Paul Celan

It's there—in the air!

It's where a pine's root
exhales Buddha's first breath, a rain drop
takes his first step.

It's where a bellowing leaf's snout
burrows beneath a mountain side's scree.

It's where a stone's light illuminates a word
falling from a glass bowl's tongue.

It's there—in the air!

It's where a wave
breaks within joined hands; within
the sheen of a tree's rings.

It's where clouds darken; raindrops
take the shape of new worlds; lives and deaths
swirl, collide.

It's there—in the air!

After the Rains Ended

After the rains ended, light
rose up from the loam
twirling around stem and leaf, illuminating
words Buddha had engraved
on bark and twig.

Wings that had fallen idle
began to beat, carrying
hope aloft; awaking
desire.

Voices began to be heard, singing in unison—

human voices, voices
of sand and stone, threshold
and sill.

It was then that a candle ignited—a newborn's sigh
emerging from its wax;
from its shadow.

PART II

"Words like us to think, and they like us to feel, before we use them; but they also like us to pause; to become unconscious. Our unconsciousness is their privacy; our darkness is their light."

—Virginia Woolf

Winter's End

In that spring's first true gleam,
lightening creased the walls
and thunder gathered the rarest of fragrances
into its mouth.

The water from my tipped bowl
spilled down a mountain the height of a weed; the breeze
read aloud evening's first page.

It was then that rain rose from the soil
and a star descended
through the roots of these words.

The evening became brighter, quieter:
no minute hand's clatter broke through;
no wheel skidded past.

I cast my lines ashore—sang as prow and sail burned,
knowing my wounds would heal.

Thoughts that had been tightly woven spun loose.

That evening's warmth lingered on my bare shoulders.
The scent of damp loam sweetened the air.

In that enormous space,
our past seemed no more than a whisper
sensed at the edge of sleep.

The Shape of New Words

Something new rises as the first rains enrich the soil:
words, believed lost, well up
past freshly shaped leaves.

A missing verse ascends through the flowering brush.

What was unfinished is ended; secrets
curl from the sky's cuff,
forming a lyric
sung by weed and stone.

Lost languages burst from a crisscross of roots,
rising through the rain's nib,
to be written on breeze and bark.

Voices that leap from a sea cliff's clay
enter our throats,
and we begin to track
the orbit of their sounds.

Forgotten pages appear in our hands.

We begin to whisper rhymes
written by the dew; by salt spray
billowing from bees' wings; by a gleam
reflected on a polished cup.

Our mouths can now shape the newest of words.

We need no longer pry them
from the fray of regretted lives, heal
their scorched hands, shelter them
from our bloodied past.

The Descent

As evening drew up I lingered outside,
waiting for what might jump
from mind to page.

I must wake the slumbering body of these words.

A stirring has begun!

At my feet, a willful phase
reshapes a patch of light.
In a thought or two, it's become a door
I swing open,
descending into the darkness.

Down I go.

Shaping my language into a ladder, I descend further.

It's quiet this far down. Still. Lovely.
I just breathe. Perfect.

But I must return.
I'm not yet ready for such peace. I can't stop
pestering my words: tapping them
on the shoulder, sorting
through their memories, unfolding
their maps.

The Seeker

My cares seemed to vanish
that mild day: fists
unclenched; clarity,
renewal.

I'd begun to sift
through clutter and symbol,
rethink my track,
ear to ground.

Rising, spirited, determined,
I knew I'd find you: breathe life
into your chalked image;

coax hope from the grit; restore
our dust-covered joys.

I soon began to sort
through phrases I'd shaped,
hunting for the right one
to wish upon.

I hadn't yet begun to wonder
which illusion I'd live: the brilliance
of our joined bodies,
or the glimpse of you
I'd dreamed.

As It Is

A wave shimmers loose from a shell's gleam,
as if to coax these words
toward open water.

As if meaning couldn't be pried
from sound; shaped by another's lips
and heard, however faintly.

As if it weren't mad
to gather images as others do shells,
pressing them forward,
line after line.

As if those images had the strength
to wield, carry—to reach
past the brain's hollow; to emerge
through a willow leaf's surge,
or a worm's skin; to whirl up
from a dog-eared page
and rest in hand.

As if that page could be borne by the wind's beak,
while its words plumbed
the source of a dream.

As if that dream were to shake me awake,
offer images chipped
from the breadth of another's sleep.

As if those images could wriggle up,
surface within my reflection;
change the way I imagine.

As if it were enough to witness
the world as it is,
and still wish to set a sea-shaped fin
on dry land.

Illusions

Something has grasped your shadow.

You can't budge. No plan. Something toys
with your adored reflection.
You'll have to give it up, set aside
what you don't need.

Let go. Your mirror
no longer fits its frame. Twist its rim,
lean further out.

So much swirls below. You want to escape—forget.

But something has begun to surge
from the dust, the flux.

It's your image! It ripples, spins.

Then, an awakening: It's no likeness. It's you
soaring above the brine.

You'd leaned out further than expected, but rose
instead of fell.

You dart and toss in the shape of your choice!

Just beyond, a breath away, a larger shape stirs.
You're puzzled. What now?

It's you, but isn't; it's there, but can't be;
but is.

It's a more perfect illusion—
beyond it,
more.

The Departure

At the very edge, we lean out further.

We're looking to return
to a narrower path; to step from a well-lit world
into the flickering light.

What a steep grade before us.
What shallowness we've endured
during these half-breathed lives.

We hope to persist, no matter:
prows pointed toward the horizon,
toward a new land.

On the edge, fear shakes its rattle—
harder, harder!

Our fingertips become stuck
beneath well-tucked corners;
between stalks and buds
too carefully arranged.

We keep questioning,
changing pace.

We've clung to more than we care to say.

What's ahead
will either sharpen our vision
or blind us.

A Light that Clings

I wake in the half-world of our time,
willing the whittle of my thoughts
into a wind-blown mask.

So much takes shape as I sift through these words.

Here's a once fallow wish
that's taken root
on my tongue's brim; a sprout
ascending through the sway of this line.

Here's a sweetness that won't recede
as I press forward; the weave
of a well-felt moment
removing a shard from my torn cuff.

Here's the sea's pitch and pull, the roiling
of winnowed dreams, a light that clings
to the mast of my thoughts.

Now and Then

The sky's crisp blue curls through me,
drawing these words
from the chaff of the world.

I'm tossing through my past's what and when
trying to rejoin its parts,
wondering whether this maple's shade
will ever cool me.

I breathe deeper, pause—try to patch
past lives together, erase chance. But so much
remains shapeless, strewn.

Perhaps it's best not to try to reweave
such frayed strands.

But I'm trying to gauge the wealth of these days.
Is it high or low?

I'm also looking ahead,
wondering which part of beyond, if any, I'll share;
or whether the shadow of this maple
fits the tree.

The Pressure

A banging emanates from within a vase. A menu
froths and snorts. A button seethes.

The handle of a pan begins to roar.

At the edge of a curb, a muddy sluice swings open.

I've tripped into it!

I'm pitching, head long. Numb.
Rungs snap. Bones
splinter.

Then—nothing. Nothing.

Then—a sigh.

I wake, as if in another's skin: part the curtain,
turn the tap,
drop a coin into the meter.

Walking swiftly, I draw strength
from evening's smallest detail,
from the husk and seed
of memory.

The beast, once again, lies trapped within its fabric.

Good enough for now.

My Slender Oars

I want to pitch out my oddly-shaped parts,
but they keep eluding me,
evading clarity.

One piece wills its way up, slips past.

Others follow, press forward,
bruising my thoughts—
having their way
with the curve of my wrist.

I dream of a beach at dawn;
fire still smoldering within circled stones.

For a moment, the blare subsides.
But soon I'm rubbed raw
by doubt.

Will this be another half-lived night?

I want to pitch these sheered bolts
before the rug comes loose,
the sand hardens.

I'm working, pulling, hoping
relief will follow,
but the past keeps unfurling,
jamming my slender oars
against the stone.

Times Like These

This is no time for excuses.

You can't seem to center yourself.
You walk on, but head down, troubled
by a worn cuff.

Your shadow languishes
as you fumble with a shoelace,
sit too close to the wall.

You thought times likes these were long past.

You want to get out, push back,
stand beneath a moonlit sky.

But where to begin?

Clouds will gather—you're sure—but where?

You imagine the rain's first moments. Your thoughts
purged of guilt and fear.

Regardless of what part
you must cut away, it's time to step up,
reemerge.

Crafting Wings

The sky seems stretched thin.

I can hear a rumbling, a growling. I've begun to adjust,
pull in my lines, set a safer speed.

People gaze past me,
as if I weren't here. No matter.

With or without a hand in mine, I sense
a great opening—a brightness.

I'll resize my hopes. Slip out,
go forward, renewed.

I'm past the high wire's midpoint, for now
no regrets.

But I'm not sure
I'll have the strength to continue
or time enough to finish
crafting these wings.

Let Death Keep

When I lowered my ear to the ground,
light burst from my fingertips
and the walls around me chimed.

I've kept my drapes tied open,
back straight, aims
well thought-out.

I can still sing a scale made from sea foam
and rice; from desire, silence.

I've etched each instant into my palm. Don't ask
what I've been
or might become—

perhaps a thread closing torn fabric,
a passing breeze.

Let death keep its precious cloak!

Each new breath
smooths my forehead,
revives hope.

Part III

"Those that truly love have roots that grow towards each other underground, and, when all the pretty blossoms have fallen from their branches, they find that they are one tree and not two."

—Louis de Bernières

That First Touch

Morning seemed unscathed,
full of desire and consent—

a sparrow above the near hedge, a breeze
cooling my opened hands.

But I knew I must ignite
those raw years
we'd shunted between us;
bury the embers.

For too long, I'd done nothing
to amend that odd story of ours,
seemingly inscribed
by another's pen.

For too long, we've gripped
a broken rung; exhaled
such tainted air.

At the edge of our divide,
we still reach out,
believing our first touch
can be relived.

I promise to begin
to be as kind as you've been
from the first,
allay your cares
in any way I can.

Back Home

I twirled a dried leaf, drawing memories
of syrup and cinnamon
from the sight of a mildewed apple
set in a porcelain bowl.

We'd decided. No more excuses.

I would linger on that stretch of beach we'd walked
one well-spent morning,
when we'd paused
to ponder our lives.

We agreed to measure
the breadth of our hopes
before casting off.

We'd first probe the light
then the larger dark,
unconcerned
with what might take shape.

Magic

Her moist lips reflect once concealed stars.

She cups her hand
around the moon's edge.

She has returned and her sighs are no longer a burden.

Her eyes were a jumble of misplaced keys.
Her lips a bird,
pecking at a snow-covered twig.

She can now sip her tea and is eager to talk.

Her fears still linger,
but the stones seem to glisten
as she steps forward.

Our New Voices

A scent, hinting of brine and beach rose, has begun to rise
from our fingertips; from the hue and tone
of well-recalled mornings.

We still share our doubts,
bear the burden of who we've sacrificed.

But it won't be long before what we've gained
becomes as true to us as light.

You've done so much to stand firm—to hold on.

What had been stunted has begun to grow wild
in our long untended places, regardless
of all we've tried to ignore.

That's the length of it—we're breaking out,
putting an end
to a narrowed dream, raising
our new voices.

Let's believe our future will out-weigh
what we can't relive.

One Step Further

A crisp memory shakes loose from my shoulders.

I step across its dream-shaped hollow,
piecing together what I can.

I see your shadow in its waters—
watch as that memory's mouth
moistens in the here and now,
becoming yours.

I'm not sure what part of our past
you'll disdain or regret
that instant I regain my balance, nor what part
you might desire to restore.

But my hope's bright skin now rests against yours.

What Joins Us

We've crossed the shallows; dressed
a spate of wounds.

Sand no longer breaches our up-turned eyes.

But what will we make of what we share? A huge room,
warmly lit? Or a paste, hardening
as the years pass?

Will our keel hold,
heady with what we've reclaimed
from torn pages?

Or regret weight down our opened hands?

We must relearn how best to speak; widen
the breadth of our words.

Come. Step forward.

I'll do what must be done. There's no undoing
that swath of luster
linking your lips to mine.

I can sense you're mending me.
You've begun to untangle that sharp-edged vine
that tightened around me;
twist open the latch
that bloodied my hand.

You've given me the will to reach up, cast off.

I'm no longer concerned with loss
or what might fade or shatter.

I'm rising to you, through it all, one step further
and I'll be there.

Our Promises

The brisk of early spring cools our neared faces.

We've begun to frame loss
and wound; judge
what to do without.

Our new portrait
includes a worn hinge,
a chipped dial—but also
a smoother blend
of color and breadth.

We've begun to set out:
sails mended; swells
lower, gleaming.

We seem weightless. The width of an echo.

I've drawn our shadows
from their hiding place, pitched memories
that obscured our path.

We've begun to press forward, unfurl
our promises.

What Never Falters

When thorns rose from the shadow of an herb,
a starling burst from these words
and a syllable's orbit
parsed a bend in my thoughts.

I continue to press the levers of sound:
hoping to animate a long-dead sigh; fathom
the curves and shapes of leaves.

I keep my sea-smoothed memories in a pouch;
renounce the surge and pitch
of asphalt; sway
as a green stalk
twists through the blade that chafes me, through the reins
that guide thought and vowel,
through what spins
and never falters.

Our Secrets

—for Frances

1

Our words have scarred our mouths.

We can't shake loose from what jabs us,
from a clutter that cuts short our stride.

Down-turned faces greet me. Tender shoots
tremble in our hands.

I'm trying to rub the soot away,
speak freely again.

I promise to cast our lines ashore,
force open the rusted gate,
if you step back,
rejoin me.

2

The stars return to their places as I quicken my pace.

My heart is ready to rise to yours,
but my thoughts remain stiff,
hard to unfurl.

Please don't offer me flowers
only the blind can heal.

The breeze has begun to ignite
long buried fragments of our days.

How quickly those losses burn!

How easy it was to retreat:
to clutch the same twig,
the same dried leaves.

Hands joined, we kneel, no longer faltering.

We find ourselves on a ledge,
neither willing to return
without the other.

Calmly, we begin to share our secrets.

Part IV

"That was the year, my twenty-eighth, when I was discovering that not all of the promises would be kept, that some things are in fact irrevocable and that it had counted after all, every evasion and every procrastination, every mistake, every word, all of it."

—Joan Didion

Second Chance

Wounds still scare the lips
of our unborn thoughts.

How often tender shoots break in our hands!

As the year begins,
we're still immersed in what separates us.
Will love reemerge?

How many branches have died!
Only a single leaf presses from the disfigured prow
of our hopes.

Where is the light we once coveted
when our table
wasn't pitted by fear?

I wish I could give you
more than this stone;
this childish drawing of a cloud.

If I could cut the sadness from me,
would there be a current strong enough
to carry it away?

Perhaps, once again, I'll be able to harmonize
with the shadow of the wind
and sing to you.

The Rudder

Stones dance to a sparrow's heartbeat.

I take the moon
from the hands of a man
who isn't holding it. Stitch it
to my sleeve.

A severed finger rises
and begins to burn.
But there is no finger, no fire.

I build a boat out of a beam of light.

I use the instant of your death
as a rudder.

The air I breathe
is also my mirror.

The Conversation

Brooding over what could have been,
a voice rises from the loam, saying:

"Don't swim that river,
the waters grow dark.
It becomes impossible to see
what darts
near out-stretched thoughts."

My heart's many voices
reply in return:

"I've become a shallow pool.
No one drinks from me. No one
watches the clouds
scud across me. Perhaps,
in the heat of a long summer
I'll disappear."

The voice replies:

"Rip that jagged bead
from your neck. Craft hope
into a pair of wings. Rise up! Seek
your radiant voice."

The Comedian

Life grabs your mirror
and smashes it on the pavement.

Pushes you down
and takes the money from your wallet.

Makes you work
until you're ready to drop—

then makes loud noises
when you're trying to sleep.

Death laughs, and says: "I'm worse.

I want to eat your memory. Watch you
forget to breathe.

How I enjoy devouring your hopes!

Many times, life turns its back,
doesn't catch you happy—
doesn't spill something on your lap.

I won't turn aside
until I've finished eating."

Messages

The hands that burst through the wall
clutch messages.

One reads:

Tear your life from its hinges. Your hopes
have become playing cards
held in vain.

Another:

Don't empty a drawer
that took so long to fill. Your life is a vase
admired more
than the flowers it holds.

Remember the years packed away, ignored.

Your future is a table
that can finally be set.

Another:

Death laughs
when he hears your name.

He's amused at the way
you try to balance
so much upon your tongue—

he's waiting for the day
it all comes crashing down.

He knows you'll make a good rung
for his broken ladder.

This is what I write
across the palms of those hands:

I wish I were the horse
in the painting on my lover's wall.

I'd be suspended above the clouds. Serene.
Lustrous.

Friends

1

I make a comet
burst from a spinning top;

put my ear to the ground,
hear the roots sing.

But the sadness
won't go away. The loneliness!

I decide to search for my death.

2

I find him among the deaths of others,
sitting on a sofa,
sipping a glass of wine.

I look into what once were eyes, hear a voice
that can't be heard:

"Don't be hurt.

What leaps from her heart
isn't love.

She uses. Plays. How long
can you be needed?

I'll never abandon you."

Venom

You've too often watched blood ooze
from splintered hopes.

You've made your bitterness
into a blade—drew it
across your tongue.

A venom gushes from the cut,
for which you claim
there is no antidote.

You built a sand castle.

Standing inside the walls,
you imagine they're made of stone;
jut high enough
to block the clouds from view.

You want to reach out, take my hand.
But it's been too long
since you last unclenched your fist.

Your muscles are rigid, painful.

The Singing

I came to a house with many doors:
because I didn't own enough freedom,
I couldn't enter.

I went to buy more freedom,
but my money was worthless.
My lungs were taken as payment.

I burrowed into the ground,
slept upon a root.

Slowly, I grew a new pair of lungs.

I pushed the soil aside one sunny day!

With my freedom in hand,
I returned to the house;
pressed the doors open,
one by one.

The house was empty! I threw down my freedom
and cried.

I was about to leave when I heard a faint sound.

The walls were singing!

The sound grew louder—my bones
had begun to sing.

I walked from the house,
fell to my knees. The dirt also sang!

I looked over my shoulder,
my freedom had vanished, in its place
a human heart.

I fit it into my chest—shaped my tattered heart
into a pillow. Fell asleep.

I woke by the sea.

The sound of the breaking waves
reminded me of the singing.

Magician

Lilac hurricanes on the moon!

Angels vanish into a spinning corpse.

Wind soughs through a stand of pine
as if through a mare's dream. Doors that were seeds
open.

I speak a language burning in the call of birds:
heard by sand; traveling
into the leaves to ripen.

I am the maker of dark things, world-weary,
working within the secrecy of the loam.

The grass is my hammer, the dusk
my moment.

Nothing stands before those rising from death:
the mountains rejoice,
beds of rivers
sing.

The Lover

1

I won't lean upon your leafless branches.

The ice on my forehead is melting.
The first green shoot
thrusts from my chest.

Soon, buds will grow from my fingertips;
birds nest within my dreams.

2

I can't remain a seed
until the seasons change.
I'll break frozen ground to reach you.

I've kicked aside a bottle
filled with messages
I was too frightened to send—

tossed off a mask
that kept falling over my eyes,
causing me to stumble
into the arms of strangers.

The Hope

I won't allow the weight
of those ruined months
to crush me.

When our hands
were farthest apart,
the shadow of that remote place
numbed me.

But thinking of how we had loved,
caused a rose to open
beneath my charred knees.

Drawing Toward You

I cherish the green leaves you lent me,
as well as the ashes.

Your touch shimmers in the wake of well-remembers nights.

I want to be the silk and stone
that guides your compass north; a kite
resting on the star of your choice.

When all the symbols have been forgotten,
all the roadmaps erased; the radiance of your smile
will still light the seaside
where I remain a pensive child.

Why should we tremble? Be separated
from the planets we love?

Stones have spoken to me. I have heard
trees' roots chime—but only you
have kept the waves
from breaking over me.

The days of my life
spread like flags on the horizon,
each one drawing me
toward you.

Breaking Point

Women fill shopping carts with stones.

A man stares at his empty hands.
Another kicks over a table
and runs from his home. A child
gasps for breath,
pacing from window to window.

Birds are born without wings.

A school of fish are found rotting
at the foot of a tree.

One war takes the shape of another,
then another.

The Alien

The moments, blindfolded, are locked
in a smoke-filled room. Months
pause in the street
to ask one another their names.

The days hurl insults at their shadows.

I open a book—no print on the pages!
I put my ear to the ground.
Nothing! Nothing!

If only I could be happy
with a new car, a machine that made
yellow balloons.

If only I could buy a new suit
and not start crying.

Surrounded

I've found a silence
that surrounds the brimming cup,
the big dinner, the new tie,
the clean shirt.

The silence isn't good or bad—and isn't going away.

I can't do anything to change it!

In the silence, I've come realize
the hollowness of names, images, places.

How threadbare the past can become.

How easy it is to stray down a track
no one else can find—

that no matter how high the jetty
the waves will be higher.

Take My Hand

I want the rain to end this silence.

I want your lips. Let me
give you this stone, once a star.

Take my hand. Someday, it may be a wing.

I want to hold you
while the night has the scent
of a lily.

I want you—before the snow
covers us. I don't want to fear
ice and frozen soil.

I want the rain to fall
because your shoulders will glisten;

because I want you to understand
our hearts have many lives.

A New Beginning

Loneliness stalked me:
jabbering, finger-pointing; hoping I'd burn
my last set of wings.

It took the shape of sandpaper, smashed candles;
became the pages of a book
molded from the dampness
of an empty house.

So many mornings
I'd wake in shoes worn thin
from retraced steps; watch a mirror
cringe as I drew near.

But you returned. Our voices
steadied, paralleled. A daisy surged
through a crack in the asphalt.

The breadth of our memories no longer wounds us.

We've filled a jar with water, tossed a line
from prow to pier, ignited
our shadows.

Inescapable

I have many hearts.

I give one to a child
born beneath the weight of a lie. Another
to a flower scorched
by the sun.

I grow wings,
fly to the ocean,
build a nest
from the bones of the wind,

shape a necklace
from each instant
of the lives I've lived
or will live.

But just above,
something vast—shadowless,
inescapable.

My breath quickens
as I ascend.

Never Again

I wish this night
could be the width of a sparrow's wing,
the weight of a pebble.

Awake. Aching. I'd become
a sheet of paper
so scribbled upon
not a fresh line could be added.

Never again!

I'm done hiding, running blindly
down a narrow path.

I've kept the dreams
you gave me:
the stones of our laughter
outweigh the tears.

Your Chalice

Stars speak to me
through a mirror stolen from death.

So what will you give me? A stone
you'd toss aside?

Or a vision of cleansed hands?

Little known corners of the day brighten me.
Fears recede.

I descend into the waves and my bones begin to glow.

All for you.

Take my secrets. My heart
is your chalice.

Full Circle

Once, like so many, I was a drawer
jammed shut.

I contained a moon,
an ocean,
a blossoming cherry tree.

But when I began to dream,
my hopes freed me.

Envoi

Another Poem

—for Richard Tillinghast

Does the sound of this poem
seem like it rises
from opened music box?

Hadn't we forgotten, so often,
to lift the lid? That its music could still be heard?

And what of the tune?

How faint it has become. So far removed
from days in that once-upon-a-time life,
when each note
seemed so vibrant.

When poems rose effortlessly
from thought to light, resolve
emanating from each line.

And the way ahead
seemed broad and truthful, its course
illuminating
our hearts.

About the Author

Joseph Murphy's work has appeared in numerous print and online literary journals, and he has authored four previous poetry collections: *The Shaman Speaks* (Middle Creek Publishing, 2019), *Shoreline of the Heart* (Shanti Arts, 2019), *Having Lived* (Kelsay Books, 2018), and *Crafting Wings* (Scars Publications, 2017). He is a member of the Colorado Authors' League and for eight years was poetry editor for a New Zealand-based online literary publication, *Halfway Down the Stairs*.

—www.coloradopoetscenter.org

SHANTI ARTS

NATURE · ART · SPIRIT

Please visit us online
to browse our entire book catalog,
including poetry collections and fiction,
books on travel, nature, healing, art,
photography, and more.

Also take a look at our highly regarded art
and literary journal, *Still Point Arts Quarterly*,
which may be downloaded for free.

www.shantiarts.com

www.ingramcontent.com/pod-product-compliance
Lightning Source LLC
Chambersburg PA
CBHW022107040426
42451CB00007B/171